# a shaft of light

*poems by*

# ANN HUANG

*Finishing Line Press*
Georgetown, Kentucky

# a shaft of light

ALSO BY ANN HUANG

*Love Rhythms*

*White Sails*

*Delicious and Alien*

*Saffron Splash*

Publisher: Leah Maines
Editor: Christen Kincaid
Cover Art: Dinosaur Skeletons by Eric Stoner
Author Photo: Greg Figge
Cover Design: Elizabeth Maines McCleavy

Printed in the USA on acid-free paper.
Order online: www.finishinglinepress.com
        also available on amazon.com

Author inquiries and mail orders:
Finishing Line Press
P. O. Box 1626
Georgetown, Kentucky 40324
U. S. A.

# Table of Contents

"... an absolute reality,
a surrealism."
André Breton

## The Words

The words to which black-and-whiteness
resurface. You are remembered. And

not to miss, amiss
floors of living dinosaurs topped out.

The shallowest and the bravest.
I will go deep under the ground
to the bottom of Grand Canyon
and hug you last.

## *Metropolis*

Holy and only,
wrenched
of familiar streams and you,
a leap from the engulfing
homebound minds.
Connected or not, you stay
not withstanding;
with your clan
you listen to heaven's frail symphony;
a legend of infused strengths;
not only
withstanding, but also
restraining.

## Prague

You're normally running behind your schedule,
The way you dance when we normally have

Two, eight, eighty people ahead,
A spectacle, a vision
A calligraphy done in brushstrokes,
next to a furnace, the mountain
As it snows hard on the strata dock,
As if you could only care less, and
Where you're normally running to
Will change the way you dance and
To be asked to
Quiet down for what will be entailed.

## In Sylvia Plath's Kitchen

A lukewarm night invites the full house
from both its past and future happiness.
Its significant attachment to all infiltrates
either the karma surrounded by it
or whom you know of the flowers
inward—moist, tender, as though they
only needed the moon.
Onward, the family shall be kindred
and intricate, inclusive without showing emotion.
Sometimes there is this exposer—exposed
more than iron-wielding stairways and drunken bedrooms. Some
traces—on top the long granite slabs, in front of the bewildered driveway—
to the hollow compartments of a soul? Mingling acts, of
dead lilt, a hospitality more than *the* hospitality,
which placed at your house
inspired these catchy fancies—those illuminations
already showing your generous attitudes to please.

## Workdays

The best of many workdays are those
    given to yours in excitement;
    the universal adversaries of our destiny
    when the half sky of thoughts undermines;.
The unhappy nights clouded by their open mic;
    the slow pains that in the light pause
    like drops from the sea; slow passions that contain
    mists drinking up life every time thunder comes!
Black as the shadow of a motorcycle ride,
    gray as a tree leaf that soaks in water,
    purple as the purest dates in a milk shake.
Those fleeting facts are of—a distinctive life
    of a distraught mind you unleashed,
    but also a reflection of our style.

## *Still Life*

Some nights

you came

through thrilling

dreams

asserting

that we had gone

through a life

of seeing

the old world

which is both

running out

and

alternating

still

## Like a Mountain

When he hugged her back

the snow drifted and the gray pastures closed down the rose buds.

He, in the crossroad, in a jean overall,

smiled with a sun above his shoulders

as the warmth oozed and ran from snow through sky.

Happiness enlarged her pupils.

Her lungs encountered the blissful wind

as the snow appeared like a mountain, humongous.

## Concussions

intake loving

                 fits in its sizes

on fitted sheets


               from all possible proportions.



the bond of two

               play mates

the ones with wings

               caress and care

for a flower's two-fold

               need to perfect.



such concussions

               inspire more than a life

aspire to more than togetherness    & ride beyond their distance.

## Moonstone

the moon elevates her eyebrows under dew

a nocturnal adoration

which undermines the surplus of myths in men's impulses

then the goddess submits to herself

amusing the moon's shiny reflection

the goddess is an deity that

prefers to submit

to her nymph-like livelihood

a beautiful creation of moonstone in fog

## *Strong*

Could it be the
humanistic features that bring
reminder to her? She
loves

that wholesome sadness
of the lyrics, she stays

re-visioning. Will they
emulate a
cautionary domesticity

from one true feeling, then
urge bodies into
a concussion of brilliance, like
the sunrise's monotonous
flames?

## *Autumn Expressions*

Autumn, a melancholy in the rose bud

without purity, the dark meteors on your face.

May you shy away from my plight and fancy,

the complete solemnity of my kindling!

A jogger, followed by Impulse and Reason,

heavenly naked, you come to Night's independence.

Many lethal hours that workout will take,

no bright hours to run adrift,

Autumn, with and without!

## Hard (Mushroom)


Rough funguses do protrude the surface—
heavenly yeast of vegetation, vertical exotic strokes, omnipotent,
tails precluding, hard-sweet in front of a courtyard
chaise, roughly standing before campers, drafting matter,
nudge-fruit, center-point. Bluff rock-rolled rather up, devil
-ish of gray, many handsome fruits turned soiled.
Your brown spots smitten under fire. The previous one, tighter,
plucked on, or for many years you have been an entertainer,
a start, a journey—the means provided for warmth and illumination;
and when you know a republic, a fake empire vanishes.

## Nomadic Yellow

If only the fire was burning. The mind

could take a breath. With circle around circle

of gusts and mist to expose the act of loving forever.

An empty museum at the center of the exit. Whether yellow

is not yellow or whose remembrance would be remembered.

When the mind is done loving, a tightened aura will engage

in the heavenly sphere. Whether many are effused to understand

that mundane incident or not. While the dew finishes

immersing and merging to earth. Yet rarely now. Life,

yellow. Nomadic yellow, life.

## *Unaware*


Swiftly the sun is drowning in the turquoise mist,

diverting himself into his own silver lap, and then

diffusing black and robust; and you in awe

know the ocean inside you, a man you did see

you wanted, and here he comes, and his loving facade envelopes your soul;

you chase him up in the valley, alluring him to stay inclined.

## *Upstairs in Real Life*

Waking up,
you raise clouded blinds
into the bright, and here we are:
sentinels, wholeheartedly in and out
of the parks, nymphlike moody birds.

Upstairs in real life you turn
slowly towards my animal-kingdom
that is obedient, absolute.
We do act. You do tease
often the sweet juicy songs up
in the big nest—more so a tease,
graciously and satisfying. Eyes, plenty.

Our nymphlike moody birds.
More letters to remark on or represent them.
We will hold onto this encounter,
which was forever this way
as if it was the last.

## Emblem

I am the one in love
and know it.
I am the one in love
comprehensively. Pray for
my big heart,
laughing and sinking with
self-deserving fortunes.
Look for my progression.
I am personable and personal,
as fatal as fate.
I give gold wishes
and shake silver seas.
I bring together
shattered
shards
of glass.
Miles of meanings.
Meanings of miles.
akin. The words
are starting to sing
and I am the investor
in all with wings.

## *The Mind Isn't a Native Tongue*


Yours is a hat painted partially without melody,
with pure sensation: childlike fancies
from spontaneity & combustion.

Given, your mind prefers an unfamiliar, unpredictable
person while no one represents quite—
hence feeling could become distinct & archaic.

The words want something from us. They enquire more.
Be that: Promise. Power house. Especially from you on Sunday.

## Short Day Half Shade

I have traveled the globe
to find
the oceans that
become melting lands when
the trees are falling, or if
it has snowed.
Look back
and then:
a girl's father
locked up
in the sanatorium
for over a year.
Many fantasies
might resurface.

## The Show

Bright, the rocks of fire,

     without a shimmer of surrounding darkness.

Now you, pursued by a midnight sun

     without the words of the beloved.

Flame, the ooze of atoms,

     secular, light without seasons,

And a reckoning of *nurses run*

     without the protest that some might see.

A shadow, your door's shade,

     hard, flattering to its circles of green—

You find the arc of civility

     and still make deals with our banal whims?

I see, young fellow.

     now, lower your ego and pray.

That's more than the lull of joy,

     The waters and streets are swayed.

## Elective Affinities

When she left

You changed
A palindrome

Which served you with
Humility
Honesty
And desire

The golden dab of water under you without
Pebble stones            the ring

A garnet line at the center illustrating

The life you discovered
After a short distraction
                    in between heaven       and home

Passings                that leaped
That would reunite

The affinity of meanings

## Footage

The pear under the dough is his dream—
Discreet elation, original like that of the moon.
The dough has cultivated his focus, his stare,
Numbly motivated, in the incline and fall
Of seeds among seeds beneath him.
He is a student of fruits and their red buds.
And he goes on keeping the seeds for himself,
The dirt absorbing him, swirling his organs,
Releasing him from the streams and their slow greens,
Elevating the candor of his heart in the moonlight.
He has a future, a bravery. New beliefs
Reside in the mist and the light of his eyes.

## Midnight Sun

The shadow nudges you.
You are soothed—
a full flower lies on the dirt road—
you rejoice.

A hard rain soaks the petal cups—
your feelings are cared for
like the rose petals.
Your feelings hold you,
you love their temperaments.
You are whole in their river.
You are whole
as the glowing corona.
The glowing corona
is held in the vase—
the leaves upright in air,
the flower cups
suspended
above their nourishing dirt:
flattened out on the hillside.

## Pictorial

The big fish
jump happily
about the bank
competing with each other
with gentle nudges
under the sky
which rears them.
And you who are happier
leaping yourself up
on both feet
all you see
are your beliefs being forfeited
and weakened with fate and age.
        There once,
the young woman who came around
dissolving your anxiety,

her focus like a thread that
was no less magical than
that of the ancestral yogis
brightening the shrine
on a workout night.

## Drilled

Too close to the cliff.
Outside a cold
cave something
is misty—timber, age,
calm without butterflies.
Sunrise and dusk,
everything is unsure—fire
which is not gold, diamonds.
which have some flaws,
and in the profile
of a moon, they
would not confuse
grass with hair.
Under the warm clouds,
what you wished for
will be drawn—
drilled.

## A fourteen-line song on loving

1.  you can avoid colors
2.  and stand still against real living
3.  you close two doors
4.  next to each other. they are called "emotional disposal"
5.  they are bewildered
6.  they are used and reused
7.  blissful and blooming et al
8.  kindred and divine hands
9.  what have you done after taking off your green pants?
10. I have made everything possible
11. sophisticated as the world
12. the mind's originality seems to prolong
13. to all who
14. love their loves

## Dynamite

The poetesses open up
a window shade that imitates
the laughter of the body
after it stops trying to please.

## In Theory

You are raised up in life by your love for peace

You then hum for humane discretion with

The pink of the air that is the pink of the words

Customs bestow on you, as a distinctive contentment

An infinite percentage of dissolving waves you take in from time

[To time]

A calming porcelain is made by space with purity?

An event of teaching, accepting and losing reality?

The view of the sky opening its unwarranted ears beneath you

(Listen)

I dream of what my life needs and am hungry.

I will catch up with your tenderness I have missed

## *Process*

In early morning's shadow, long
night would be gone,
the leisure retired underneath it
—whatever that might be—

leaves of a new world
under the same database:
could you unleash that:
redo a window coverings of
minimal finials?

*

Minimal time when
entries without maps
find it: *I Ching,*
Chinese philology, the ideals
for life from synchronicity
in German: temporal,
when Nietzsche lashes out
at sophisticated scholars
from continual agnates

and at last they see arduous earth.

## Elective Affinities II

Even if life goes by sometimes
Less charmingly
Than many of its hot cheat sheets
In a world infiltrated by
Man's ignorance, by lay politicians
With their seeded greed
Then
Ouch,
Mother Theresa
Lies down with hunger breaths.

## *Untitled*

The devil flirts with a woman:
"Mme, you're cute!"
"And," responds the woman,
"This reality of your eternal lie
makes me aware of
The possibility of your presence."

## Variable Life

Be a happenstance.
I capture your mind as a film poem
Exposed in experience, for I always see
How happy you will be without losing me at last.
You want me more when
I extend your company to its meaningful end.
Out of passion lower my strong knees- and come-.

## *Poems for Mothers*

Your mother swings around the bed post,
which bruises her leg.
For you know it takes place
where she is careless, and
a mother's body
propels a daughter's feeling.
Your mother laughs in spite of her tears;
you provide some balm for her limb.
It is the beginning of that.
Square or square: now and ever.
You love learning from her propensity for danger.
She loves learning from your healing.

## Crustacean

You had gone out of the state, beyond havens of flowers,
Backing a voluptuous sea.
Something stayed—hummingbirds hovered and left,
Moon and confections lurked
Where the sore nose was after you
And the hurting knees,
Bent down under a bed,
Listening behind a wall.
The woman in bed
Reappeared in the water.
That was a love scene for one life.
More things would remain.
The air would never rise, and then rise,
And the hummingbirds sing.
The clouds would never be the same gray
Lime on the horizon.

And you were lying like a shaman
Amid the neat firm night,
Your nose near the blue pillow,
Which makes our promises real.

## Continental

Whenever she reproaches you with nothingness,
or elevates you onto her rabbit's foot,
given you have the key of seeing, you redeem love
and alienate yourself from her customs.

Her serenity travels like air into your lungs,
leaving you weak and wary of her love.

Her frailty calms you like fireworks.
Bright-hearted you dream of rewinding years,
adoring her vast bamboo trees
beyond the sound of Space's divine steps, if
only melting ideals into the sun.

## Woodworking

While our space, a luxuriating cabin, grabbed us
with solid walls and mosaic hexagon glasses,
you knew I was not there yet.
You knew I would have fought for you against
someone who had done you injustice
or thought there was more need for crayons
or that my jumpsuit wasn't cool or storied
or something opened
our beliefs in fullness.
While the chances for us only left...
you wished I could stop at your woodwork,
which reunited our dreams
of previous nights.

## Sense Poetics

To have not
many
whimsical instances
of loving
the one
without loving oneself
I do seldom see
or think
from the interior

of the myopic
re-visioning of the providence
I might include
uncertainty of a
strong pulse

by the mountain's door
at the wood's edge
go for the woman

in smooth romper
dressed for life
who wins over

the certainty
of death.

## Your Life

You had a life
to bring to the silver lake
in a forgotten way . . .
water
thinned and white
as the drained age of poppy seeds . . .
castle
left alone in saffron banks . . .
sky
translucent as a happy whale . . .
and the urgent moon
splurging all its silver
over New Zealand, gin-pure, merging into the sea . . . )
And the night is one upside-down after another
or its moon a glory of black lures
glued-in
acute-blue sky

When could you own your life?

## Frozen Dream

An orange, orange. A guava, guava. A pearl, pearl.
Yes. The art of all, a given.
Orange is orange or guava is guava or pearl is pearl.
And all is not what is given, but what it gives.
What they give is what they are given to.
And how you perceive is more than it is.
The meat of the orange is guava and pearl.
Because the meat of the orange gives, to you, the orange.
The color of the guava beats none but guava.
The guava you know is the guava guavas compete with.
An orange is an orange that is orange, and more so.
Pearl is the name given for its color, not like other pearls.

## *Anywhere*

Anyone anywhere falls
a bit later than me after
the boldest beaming orange,
the brightest bright, strengthens
with light the mind
soothed by morning pelicans

close relatives or lovers
who have known her
moon-tooth
childlike voices out of a warm stream

A wanton daydreamer
procures nightly poetry-writing artistry without
preemption
up one flat
then down three stairs

anywhere

## Film of Bodies

For you are a girl, the keenness towards wisdom
is nor on your trajectory, not are the film of bodies
on my head, the surroundings of November, flowers
falling from the dry sky
out of marble stone. "A body
might be wise
inside out," I write today.
When you rewind the film,
the statues are there. From the east,
we are freeing a statue from a plaza or adding it to
her heart excitable in front of a mass
of people. Her statue, replica
of gain, shrinking slowly
around her passion.

## Cranberry Sun


Cranberry sun for you, this morning.
Cranberry sun. This large field listens
while you take in and enclose it. You play by ear,
from commanding this morning.
Stories are in your waking grandchildren's essence
this morning. You believe the world of stories
only while you know the cranberry sun, more so when you're humbled.
That's about idleness—and a shaft of light.
If only humans did not recreate.
Relationships mending boredom.
The famine right behind you.

## Sun by Your Mother

Sun that does not discern mother's
Denial and lesser endings,
Sun stamped emptiness
without your soul.
Those aren't your mind's distant echoes,
Failure of many of your mindsets,
Stamping, shattered, re-negating
Fruits of many of your mindsets.
Those aren't your tangent centers
Stopping in my endings.
Letting go souls from mothers,
Swimming in with your endings,
Sun of your mother, and daughter.

## The Nightmare

Do appreciate.
The nightmare is mine
or it is not mine in its diminishing truths.

Falseness of all sorts,
from letting go of the low delving into it
to the opened bridges.
The bridges around my legs will break,
Somehow they get stuck,

Do appreciate.
And later,
later set me free!

Since the destiny became derelict and stale,
the bridges see,
the water beats every night without complaint,
every morning the mouths of the creeks take in themselves, alluring...
characters of the Nightmare,
your moon and drought and wind,
all leave slowly.

## Canvas Replicas [by Matisse]

Many mornings
when there wasn't a shiny sun,
you stood still
to sing songs
about birch tree buds.
And the puzzle of morning beams
outside the blink
you illuminated,
But you couldn't even sing for
whom you loved.
For before the beginning of your songs
You haven't decided my being.

## SCARCE

The thought of the universe is expanse,
Short and unanimous. Seeing,
Not loving and loving;
Overly taught;
Women and dogs
left fumbling,
And scarce.

## Life/Crime

Your daughter would lie down
on soil. Your son wondered how
the window got opened in front of you.
And where you came from
left you already. My hands
did a favor to your waist,
their poetics a plate for the future.
You darling, you darling, back on track.
Then there was all love involved.

## Summer Flowers

Their simple directions
of the attending and
the absenting are half way given—
a dry sun
ran swiftly after
the narrow bushes,
their leaves tilt towards the sun
by a serendipitous summer
the flaming buttercups
awakened from the heat.

## Indelible Winter

Your shout out to the flowers, the flowers,
"I will not keep wishing
Isn't platonic."
Rainy moon infiltrates into air decreasing in liquidity
You can't take control of your heart
or about stories. Your hands touch. Gray contemporary
weep you see wind-
fall, your noticeable shirt protruding
a swift rebirth. All the more so you see
from the flowers, almost, their ever-growing power.

## Then

In my one love that received eternality!
Few had sprung before,
None had come after.
Thus I did best in the past, —dispersing
Out of the apertures of calmness.
Emotions and ideas and spirit and sensibility—
Paralleled in a way that left you foremost all this time,
Me in front of you, me above you, beside you—
You—perhaps in addition to present space, future space,—
That tag of our love-space's many instances I missed!
How briefly did such lingering stay? Tender—
The interior space—more than that—
Where climatic fists lavished fondling you all at once!

## After Obama

You have shown me the torch
to where presidents lie laureled in the mountains
in the gold-black storm, many swirling in white karma.
They have gone forward and only few visionaries
        unite people for their countries,
for there are countries bringing the storms to the floor.
You have run out of time,
You have gone on with the old ticket
        and now you lean on the progression of aura.

## A Light-Hearted Promise

My light-hearted promise
has been familiar to you;
and sometimes when you see life in the rearview mirror,
when you duck down to the roots of waking,
when you stay calm with scotch,
There you see my heart.

## *Love*

Love is a beach outside the windows, a full bridge,
    For whom it receives at the opposing end of giving;
Love buys the humble mind's altar to Chance.
    They have seen the beloved, who detest pride. More so
Where two bodies, hungry one another, discover shaking,
    And blissful moments, and echo the laughing
Of incredulous behavior, on earth—and make
Their imaginary grand lives beyond their kisses, and keep
All in her otherworldly days, all without a breather.
    Many can't hold on to those days. And they see love become stale,
Become diminished infinitesimal, which was the only bitter truth.
    Bewilderment is always around the foot and neck,
And it brightens, and lives through touch about touch.
Some of this isn't enough; and some of love isn't all but this.

## Bond

That's either black
or salty.
That does welt
after bending over,
unbroken and hardened
for it can see
joy,
longing,
reclusiveness.
That has
a locale to aim for.
More than a holder
of tentacles,
ginormous,
loud. Wavy,
you see it outside
its house pleading
a bright birthmark:.
you need—

and you can lose it:
there's no lock.
You can smear it
on your skin
and show me to
the tip of it
how you feel. There,
all mine, then—
and you'd better
make me so,
too.

# Raw Stitches [Zelda's Hat]

after F. Scott Fitzgerald's *Tender is the Night*

A consequence and all the way, a consequence and silent enough, a consequence minus a silent voice and minus a silent collapse and a humbled car, a signage of minus, a wound and a small wound and an unsettling feeling and madness, a chunky beige hat and a big tie.

## Stallion

You will take off those shoes gray
And run by the bay till it's notoriously
Colorful
Wearing the shoes bright
Running over a bliss that's not been felt by me
The shoes will take you
You had been fighting under the cave
By leaving your name

## A Flower Among Blooms

The show curated by the art director
sinks
deep under the earth and floats up; the
shrine
Is orange as an air in a nursery; your
shadow,
unlike dots of low shadows next to a pillow, ends the
morning
laughter that welcomes the mornings
so quiet, foreign, and non-recurring from the past.

## Iconic Ironies

The ocean-bound chiseled nose,
The square-shaped nursery's facade,
The softness from sparks from my waists
Always imposing truth onto dignity;
The measures of Syndicate, _____ and the book of Jesus
Appeared more than the shadows penetrating
Depth beyond the wind
Of Iconic Ironies.

# Firmament

From ~

In appearance you stayed with one solid Being,
so bright in light that the Morning painted delight,
mainly without keenness at places of such substance;
or as you knew your heart beat on and on
in heartfelt transport through ginormous weight of sea,
from the first tissues of the wondrous Roots,
where lightest clouds are bound to reason:

now, some unity on your own Heaven is deemed at Work!
And the healthy belief that I was close-by
maintaining unpleasant forgetfulness that I was far from,
who ought to be, placed on a local venue,
more than a Need from you, as night by night
your love unforgiven, caring all that may
escape from that Home stayed quotidian.

## *Two Lovers*

As you stand by desk,
Vertical on your feet,
There show through your window
Some visible scenes of peoplehood—
Slow runs of task-driven adults, others
Innocence in their wandering walks,
Servant and woman in sunbeam spring's morning,
Men in their gray suits with coffee mugs in their cold hands,
Young women talking loudly to the sunshine
From the Now. And me
Leaving you heartaches while letting our future go.

## Wonderful

Why did my mother lend her hands to you
When you needed them;
Or embrace, or open up,
So that you would merely be able to launch
Yourself my way?
Why does she resonate with your likeness
And toughen with mine?
Why can't you free me?
Should you accept it all?
From doing me no justice,
Or leave me a breadth of recurring bitterness
From generosity and sweetness
Under her watch
While I write?

## *Beyond Reach*

You've already seen me.
It is a Sunday
In Cape Cod.
The water brews hastily.
There is a bottle full of letters
Under a boat not far from the dock.
Personal scribbles
Are shaded
Behind beams of light
And then you find my gaze.

## *(The opera in exhaustion)*

(The opera in exhaustion) (submitted by) (soulful attendance)

    (He won the cases) (on (narrow remarks)) (practically        forgettable)

        (Counsel descend)

(Ignoring) (the significant) (disadvantage)    (compelling sex    scenes)

    (Forfeiting premises)        (You find the sea urchin)

(Directions towards a living within)    (that could be yours)    (a sun within the egg)

        (Directions towards mountains) (and they are the ones without hassles)

        (In the humility of your (practical manhood))    (you have not made (noises)  during (true moments))

        (By meaning (actually))

    (An artist) (eludes the benefits from a living within)

## Poem

Distance and dimension, as poets write,
Are deeds that can be beaten.
The bees that migrate one season
Have died on their arrival.
We allow them to die where they may,
When time and survivorship are costly,
For life is life; and it ends.
Poets agree.
The weeds you gave me when dryness
Was affecting the buttercup.
May the weeds of life be many
And may they be kind.

## Untitled

In Peace, if Peace be Peace, if Peace be yours,
Religious and unreligious could be unequivocal forces:
Unreligious in some is needed by religious in many.
    That isn't the big leak in the pipe,
It has mundanely made the words silent,
Or somehow bridges the void sharply.
    That big leak within the husband's pipe
And big ambiguous scents of fresh linens,
what is damaging outward swiftly heals inwardly.
    *That is worth the wait: allow it come:*
*And should it say, sunshine, say, yes.*
*Or be beguiled somehow and some more.*

## T. Cartilage

There we come
shadows high and short
under the spell
beyond noon and midnight
Sometimes once
a simpler wish
one then's
one now's
one identity
mine and the only one
and mine
enlarged into a sky wall
the quintessence of which
holds the moon

## Gaia

I.

Meadow, stern meadow
formed tip in sea,
gaia, fortress fruits,
two ecosystems extra terrestrial
are balanced,
or I paint light like a chunky cloud.
Unlucky ones,
beloved and loving,
tender myth-push,
sweet-fruit,
bitter and sugary—I am water
in your mouth.

II.

Doesn't the woodworker
move me as he approaches?
Doesn't my head merge time
to the sea?
Haven't we abandoned time before us—
periods of time?
Evidence of gaia—fruits
under the dirts,
I am painted purple,
painted like submarines
that remain beside the sweet gaia.

## The Rising Waves

Spring is underneath the short waves that leave us,
Or underneath the plateau in the parsley fields;
Magenta the waves of the dew under you,
Or magenta the dry sweet-honeydew melons.

The day of the dissipating of love has beheld you,
strong and simple is your blissful heart;
Mind you stay, joyous the reason of lust,
Without a touch or a nudge on my ring finger.

## The Peace in Black & White

The print book on the floor

disguises the contemporary peace

in B&W:

China in black

Japan in white

US in black

Russia in white

Mexico in black.

The peace

on the book

is blissfully

stupid

or B&W.

## The Inspiration

Then, added on that first seductive hug,
which refreshed two bodies, and suffocated them afterwards;
stay this form, and made you stay there,
   or made yourself beat your toughest nights.
You wondered some to de-love; and had you own
   one life as luxury as dreams, "Come,"
come; or whether this world had already saved me,
   tightened you with love, by allowing you come.
And, whether it had, made your world turn against you,
   Or an unbeknown home for a savior.
Now it would be just in time to save you,
   to be simply alive, coming and allowing, "Come."

## *A Lifetime*

The trees have done a dark circle
  About the lake beneath.
The high moon is racing up
  Under a clear night.

Who do I contemplate to make my heart pound so hard,
  Or let go my tears?

## Plain Air

Mist above the drying land.
Red mist. Land not deemed for living.

Emerald diffusion to be dissolved,

Flowers meant to be spoiled. There
Is a plate, a fork, a glass, a fissure.

Dead legends, somebody and you

From somebody and you only: fallen,
Catch. Why aren't we ready?

## Proverb and Prodigal

*—after Carl G. Jung's Red Book*

A purple line about your mind where
you sing a song "ocean of time"

Ocean of time:
   to welcome the night by leaving it out
      from the day

You envisioned the world "power" & knew
   how to glue it onto the fortune wheels
   Ginormous, young child and alive:
      to let go the mushiness of a mushroom
         after it hasn't been picked

by the clinging skin

showing off the kin's
portraitures

beyond the eclipse when moon/sun are separated from each other
I can feel it singled out by their simple lives

when the whole of you receives the light

# ACKNOWLEDGMENTS

I would like to express my most sincere appreciation to these people:

First and foremost, to my editor and friend Leah Maines for her steadfast and personable skills, great tastes in poetry, and trust in me ... and above all for her constant designs and inventive ways and her understanding of what my poetry conveyed within the confines of today's day.

To my generous teacher and friend Leslie Ullman for so expertly guiding my writing career with paintings and mix-media composure with unsurpassed dedication and personal care. For her tireless dedication and undivided attention to the craft and details of my work.

And to my passionate mentor and friend Ralph Angel for his wise counsel and for being a role model of grace and professional growth.

To the entire team at Finishing Line Press, I would like to express my deepest appreciation for believing and trusting in me over the years, especially to Christen Kincaid and Jacqueline Steelman, for overseeing all facets of the publishing process with great responsiveness and seamlessness. A very special thank-you as well to Elizabeth Maines, and Kevin Maines for their unending support and patience.

My utmost thanks as well for the tremendous support of my brilliant teachers Jean Valentine, Richard Jackson, and Rigoberto Gonzalez in the college stretch and to my workshop leaders, Larry Sutin, Domenic Stansberry, Jody Gladding, Jen Bervin, and all of the amazingly talented people who make up the Vermont College of Fine Arts.

To all of my devoted publishers, my most heart-felt thanks for their beliefs and efforts to place my poems under their umbrella, on making of these quintessential poetry books.

To my imaginative and talented friend and photographer Eric Stoner for taking so many dynamite photos for my many ongoing poem-film projects, to whom I am in debt for this book's cover photo.

To my keen and imaginative social media expert Theresa Holland for watching over my social media, blog pages and web messages.

To my dedicated and inventive digital guru Curt Cuscino for overseeing my poetry site and all things virtual.

To my husband, Josh, for continuing to share with me his passion for art, his persistent inventive flare, and for keeping my feet on the ground when things strike.

And finally, I would like to express my gratitude, love and respect to my parents—Xiao Ling Hou and Da De Huang—for letting me dream big and being the one I always dreamed to be.

**A**nn **Huang** is an author, poet, and filmmaker based in Newport Beach, Southern California. She was born in Mainland, China and raised in Mexico and the U.S. World literature and theatrical performances became dominating forces during her linguistic training at various educational institutions. Huang possesses a unique global perspective of the past, present, and future of Latin America, the United States, and China. She is an MFA candidate from the Vermont College of Fine Arts. Her surrealist poem "Night Lullaby," was a Ruth Stone Poetry Prize finalist. "Crustacea" another of her surrealist poems, was nominated Best of the Net in Priestess & Hierophant. In addition, Huang's book-length poetry collection *Saffron Splash,* was a finalist in the CSU Poetry Center's Open Book Poetry Competition. **Ann Huang** is also the author of the award-winning poetry series *Love Rhythms, White Sails,* and *Delicious and Alien.*

www.annhuang.com

www.ingramcontent.com/pod-product-compliance
Lightning Source LLC
Chambersburg PA
CBHW021155090426
42740CB00008B/1108